How to Beat Granddad

at Checkers

Revised Edition

By John P. Cardie

Illustrated by Bob Murr

How to Beat Granddad at Checkers - Revised Edition
is written by John P. Cardie
illustrations by Bob Murr
Copyright © 2008, John P. Cardie

Published and Printed by:
Lifevest Publishing
4901 E. Dry Creek Rd., #170
Centennial, CO 80122
www.lifevestpublishing.com

Printed in the United States of America

I.S.B.N. 1-59879-598-8

Table of Contents

Author's Aim

It is the goal of the Author to have as many young children as possible get involved in playing Checkers and to learn the beneficial "Lessons of Life" it teaches. Although underrated, this granddaddy of all board games, is simple to learn, yet, very intense. Checkers helps children to cultivate "critical thinking skills" and is vastly superior to chess in improving a child's forethought. Enhancing a child's foresight lessens their chances of making poor choices as teenagers and young adults. My hope is to spearhead a national "revival" of Checkers at the expense of violent video games and other sinister games like "Texas Holdem Poker" that encourages addictive gambling.

Checker playing can be a stimulating - interactive - multi-generational - challenging and inexpensive pastime that builds important social skills and it's **FUN!**

"There's more to Checkers than pushing plastic"

Cardie Checker Clan

Foreword

It has been said "No greater love has a man than this – that he give up his life on behalf of his friend". A man's* life consists of his <u>time</u>. When he runs out of time, he runs out of life. Therefore, any Granddad* who gives his Grandson* his time is giving him the "Greatest of Gifts".

Many famous men who have achieved "greatness" in the world's eye have done so at the expense of their son's life. So much of these men's lives was spent acquiring their "greatness" that they neglected spending <u>time</u> on properly rearing their offspring. That is sad!

Fortunately, many Granddads are now blessed with having a chance to correct earlier child rearing mistakes by spending more time with their <u>Grand</u>sons than they did with their <u>own</u> sons. Not only do Granddads have more "free time", but they also have more knowledge to share and give. Giving shows true love, and that is something all Grandsons crave.

It's been said, "Experience is the best teacher". It should be, considering it costs the most. However, I believe it's better to learn from others experiences, especially the negative ones. It's dumb to learn from your own experience that driving fast on icy roads is not safe. It is smarter to learn this from some dimwit's mistakes, right?

Smart Grandsons, while sitting across a checkerboard for hours with Granddad, can quickly learn from Granddad's past experiences. Granddads can teach him where the piles of dog-dirt lie along life's pathways. He knows where they lie because he stepped in so many of them over the numerous past decades.

Finally, studies have shown that Granddads who play Checkers reduce their chances of getting Alzheimer's. Also spending time with children helps keep old folks "young at heart", so it's a win – win situation for both parties. It's time for Granddads and Grandsons to start having these "board meetings" as soon as possible.

*Purely as a matter of convenience, male pronouns are used throughout this book. Certainly these principles apply to Grandmothers and Granddaughters equally as well.

"There's more to Checkers than pushing plastic"

Chapter 1

Questions and Answers

Question 1 – Why should I learn to play Checkers?

Answer 1 – Studies have shown that it will improve your math scores in school. It helps you think logically and solve problems easier. It also aids in developing self-responsibility and improves your concentration skills. These traits should help you make more money later in life.

Learning to play Checkers well is the fastest way to develop foresight. This ability of being able to see and plan ahead will surely help keep you from making dumb mistakes later in life. You'll make better life-choices and avoid a lot of needless pain and suffering, than if you did not have such keen fore-thought.

Playing Checkers is inexpensive and doesn't require batteries or a computer. With a little practice, and help from Granddad, you can easily be "School Champion", defeating most chess and computer geeks who haven't studied this oldest of all board games.

Lastly, playing Checkers is **FUN!**

Question 2 – What is the quickest way to learn how to play Checkers?

Answer 2 – Go to your Granddad and use the four magic words. They are "I need your help". For some strange and unexplainable reason, 60+ year old Granddads did not grow up playing video games, but most of them know how to play Checkers. Just ask, they won't say no as they understand that checker players are always "On-the-square". Just try asking, it works well.

Question 3 – What's in it for Granddad?

Answer 3 – Granddads love to show off for their Grandsons. Most don't pole vault or slam dunk a basketball anymore, but enjoy doing something to prove they can still beat kids at something. Playing Checkers makes them feel special. Also it's been suggested that playing Checkers helps prevent Alzheimer's and dementia. Furthermore, it's one of the few things that Granddad can still enjoy and indulge in, and it's salt, caffeine, cholesterol and fat free.

Question 4 – What if Granddad says that he's too tired or busy?

Answer 4 – Ask him if he would prefer you…

1. Go next door to your hoodlum neighbor's house and spend the afternoon playing violent video games while listening to profane Rap music?

or…

2. Spend time learning to play "Texas Holdem Poker" so you can be addicted to gambling for life?

or…

3. Watch soap operas all afternoon while eating bags of potato chips?

Don't worry, he'll soon be blowing off the dust from his old board and saying…."Now here's how to play, sonny".

Question 5 – What if Granddad has forgotten the official rules of Checkers?

Answer 5 – He can refresh his memory by reading the "Standard Checker Rules" in chapter 7 in this book. Afterwards he can take you to McDonalds and order a Fillet of Fish sandwich to help keep his memory strong. My son informed me that if I ate more fish my memory would expand, but that may not be true. After eating "Pepperidge Farms" cheddar cheese Gold Fish™ crackers every day for 3 months, the only thing that increased was my waistline.

Question 6 – How can I have fun while Granddad is teaching me all the rules?

Answer 6 – Suggest to Granddad that he give you a nickel for every time you jump one of his men. The most it will cost him is only 60¢ per game. Even someone on Social Security can afford that. Long before he spends $15 you'll know how to play and will have enough money to buy yourself some ice cream and your Granddad a fish sandwich for teaching you this wonderful game.

It's the best investment he'll ever make.

Question 7 – How can I enjoy that "winning feeling" as a beginner?

Answer 7 – That's easy! Use this method. After you've learned the rules, play Granddad a game straight up, twelve against twelve. If he wins, remove one of his back row Checkers before the next game. If he wins that game, too, remove 2 back row Checkers before the next game. Keep removing one more of his Checkers for every game lost. Before long, you'll be enjoying a win and will learn the value of trading pieces once you're ahead. Now, after winning, put one of Granddad's Checkers back on the board for the next game. This method will also make the games more challenging and entertaining for Granddad.

Question 8 – How can I learn to beat Granddad the quickest way possible?

Answer 8 – As in most games, practice makes perfect and perfect wins. There is a perfect <u>time</u> to move the perfect <u>checker</u> in the perfect <u>direction</u>. Studying books on the way great Grand Masters moved and why, is a great method for improvement. Studying Checker Puzzles also helps, as well as playing against a computer or fellow Checker players on-line (see chapter 8 for info on these subjects).

However, if you learn the Checker tactics and pitfalls outlined in this book, you will easily beat most players your age, as well as most Granddads.

"There's more to Checkers than pushing plastic"

Chapter 2

True and False Quiz

1. True or False
Chess is older than Checkers.

False: According to historians, Checkers is more than twice as old as chess.

2. True or False
An official checker board is red and black

False: The official colors are green and buff (off-white).

3. True or False
The official tournament colors for Checkers are red and black.

False: They are red and white. These colors, played on the green squares have been shown to produce the least amount of eye strain during the long hours of tournament play.

4. True or False
A standard rule in Checkers is that RED moves before WHITE at the beginning of every game. The reason is that in America, the RED men (Native Americans) moved here before the WHITE men (Europeans).

False: It's true that RED does move first, but not for the reason given above.

Refer to the numbered board illustrated at the end of this chapter for questions 5, 6 and 9.

5. True or False
Playing from the RED side, your best opening move is 11 to 15 and the weakest move is 9 to 13.

True

6. True or False
It is a weak move for RED to vacate a checker on his King row early in the game.

False: Moving the checker on square 4 early in the game is a strong move.   Standard openings like…Black Doctor, Bristol, Cross, Double Corner, Dyke, Old Fourteenth, Paisley, Single Corner, Souter, etc. all make this move early in the game.

7. True or False
The following "famous" men all played and promoted Checkers and never considered it a waste of time to study this "Grand old Game"
      1. Alexander the Great
      2. Napoleon Bonaparte
      3. King Edward VIII of England
      4. Abe Lincoln
      5. General Ulysses S. Grant
      6. Teddy Roosevelt
      7. Andrew Carnegie
      8. Peter Lashkevich
      9. Jack Dempsey
      10. Edgar Allen Poe
      11. Dr. Marion Tinsley
      12. Harry Houdini

False: Peter Lashkevich was my Grandfather, he wasn't a checker player or famous.

There is a lesson to be learned here. 11 of the 12 men listed were both famous and played Checkers but one did not. Failing to notice the danger in just <u>one</u> of your opponent's Checkers can lead to a defeat. Diligence in examining <u>every</u> checker your foe has before making your move is one key to success.

8. <u>True or False</u>
When you play any American Checker Federation (ACF) tournament you can make any legal move that is possible on your opening play.

<u>False:</u> Most tournaments today use the ACF 3 move restriction deck of cards consisting of 156 different openings. Go as You Please (GAYP) where there is no restriction produces too many draws among the master players.

9. <u>True or False</u>
It is sound strategy for the RED side to attack WHITE's "Closet" double corner (squares 28 and 32) as RED most often gets his first King there.

<u>True</u>

10. <u>True or False</u>
Chess is like the Everglades, and Checkers is like the Grand Canyon.

<u>True:</u> Chess, like the Everglades, is vast and wide but not very deep. Rarely can you force your opponent to move 3 consecutive times in a row. Checkers, like the Grand Canyon, is profoundly deep and unfathomable. Master players often think dozens of moves ahead. This foresight ability is not possible in chess because there is no forced capture.

11. <u>True or False</u>

Nowadays people who are knowledgeable about computers are called geeks. Sixty years ago, people who were knowledgeable about Checkers were called "Wood Pushers".

<u>True:</u> Today more than 99% of all Checkers are made of plastic. Therefore today's checker players could rightly be called "Plastic Pushers".

12. <u>True or False</u>

You should be an "expert" at Checkers before teaching it to children.

<u>False:</u> You don't need to be "Lance Armstrong" to teach a kid how to ride a bicycle.

13. <u>True or False</u>

Playing Checkers is like working a crossword puzzle with a pen instead of a pencil with an eraser.

<u>True:</u> That's why playing Checkers is harder than Chess! In Chess, except for the Pawn which must advance, you usually have the option to erase (take back) your poor move on your next turn.

"There's more to Checkers than pushing plastic"

Superman Loves Checkers

Superman loves Truth, Justice, and the American way – that's his motto. Checkers promotes <u>truth</u>, the quality of being righteous. Poker players often bluff, but checker players are always on the square. Checker's rules are <u>just</u> – you win by skill, not luck. Games using dice, cards or spinning numbered wheels involve chance – not savvy and expertise. Therefore, any Bozo can win if "Lady Luck" smiles on him. Superman doesn't rely on luck or play the lottery. He knows that's dumb.

Checkers instills the <u>American democratic way of life</u>, while chess endorses the <u>discriminatory caste system</u>. In chess, all pieces must give their lives to save the sacred King. The lowly pawn can never, ever become a King no matter how hard he works. However, in Checkers any ordinary, commonplace piece, can aspire to become a King if it works hard and progresses to the finish line. It is the American dream, come true in a board game. No wonder Superman loves it!

"There's more to Checkers than pushing plastic"

The numbered board

WHITE

32	31	30	29
28	27	26	25
24	23	22	21
20	19	18	17
16	15	14	13
12	11	10	9
8	7	6	5
4	3	2	1

RED

Chapter 3

Basic Strategy

Checkers is a War game. The army with the last man standing (or in Checkers, the side making the last move) wins!

Each army (side) consists of 12 soldiers (Checkers). The battlefield is the checkerboard and neither side has a material advantage. The first tactic or goal is to control the "top of the hill" on the battlefield. In Checkers, this is the center of the board. Having your Checkers control the board's center is like having your soldiers on top of the hill on the battlefield. This is known as a "positional advantage". Soldiers on top of the hill can throw their stones or shoot arrows farther than their enemy down below. In time, your men will kill or capture one of theirs, giving you a material advantage. In a checker game, a checker in the middle or center of the board can kill to the right or left, but a checker against the side of the board is like a one armed soldier, he can only kill in one direction. So the first strategy is: Always try to control the middle of the board by moving or jumping towards the center.

The second strategy is to start trading man for man once you are a checker ahead. Why? Because trading man for man magnifies your material advantage.

Consider These Facts:

Twelve against eleven Checkers is only a 9% advantage, but two against one gives you – 100% advantage, twice the strength. Two kings against one is almost always a victory, unless you move into the sandwich trap, which is easy to avoid, or have your two Kings held by one King in the single corner.

Here's how it works. Once you gain a checker by doing the Snake Eyes trap or the Meatless Sandwich trick, start sacrificing your Checkers one for one or two for two. As the General of your army, you kindly place your arm around Soldier Sam and say "Sam, for the good of our team you must take your sword, run down this hill and kill one of the enemy." He'll probably say, "But if I do that, I'll die". He is correct, but that's part of War. Next, put your arm around Corporal Conrad; give him the same order as you gave Sam. Do the same with Private Pedro, Lieutenant Larry, Sergeant Sean, etc. until there are only two of you left and one of your enemy. At this point you both go down the hill and finish him off, winning the battle. So in a nutshell, the winning strategy in Checkers is the same as in chess or in a real life war. Gain a positional advantage and this will give you a material advantage. Once you obtain that, trade to magnify this advantage and start planning your victory march.

So how do I get control of the top of the hill – the center of the board? Here's a proven method. First, look at a numbered board and assume you're playing red. Try to go as far into the game without moving the six Checkers in your "pyramid". Which are they? They are the Checkers on squares 1, 2, 3, 6, 7 and 10 when playing RED or squares 23, 26, 27, 30, 31 and 32 when playing WHITE.

WHITE pyramid

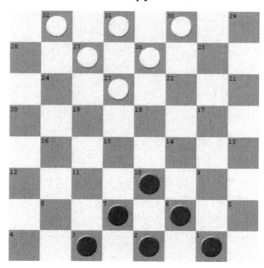

RED pyramid

11

This will give you "Pyramid Power", a structure as tough to break down as the pyramids in Egypt. The other six Checkers you have should be used to break down your opponents pyramid by trading them off. Many new players are fearful to move out checker #4 from their back row (King row) for fear that the enemy will get a King. That's foolish thinking. Don't be afraid to get this guy into the fight early. By doing so, in a sense you have an extra soldier if your opponent is unwilling to get his single corner back row man into the fight. This is often enough all the advantage you need to gain a checker up on your opponent early in the game. From there you simply trade your opponent down to his demise.

If, however, you find that you must move a pyramid checker, start with square 10. As the game progresses, 7 and 6 must get into the fight. The two Checkers you should try really, really hard not to move are numbers 1 and 3. These two Checkers form what is called a "Bridge". If you don't move these two Checkers, your enemy cannot get a "King" without help.

The above "War Plan" should give you an overall plan of attack and a reason or purpose behind every checker you push.

Finally, one very important tip – ***never take your eye off your enemy.*** Against a strong player, making just one mistake can bring defeat. You can't unscramble an egg. Once you have moved a checker, you can never take it back. You snooze; you lose. You must always first look at your enemy's Checkers, not yours. You must see what harm he is trying to do to you before you can start thinking how you can hurt him. Always think defense first – then offense. An old saying goes, "As soon as you see a great move, sit on your hands." Why? - Because you're not thinking defense first. Your enemy may be giving you that "free" checker because he's planning to later take two of yours. In chess this is called a "gambit". Remember, in chess you can make a bozo move and still have time to recover. Whereas in Checkers, just one careless oversight is all it takes for a Granddad to say "Na-Na-Na-Na-Nana – I beat you again". Who wants to hear that?

"There's more to Checkers than pushing plastic"

Chapter 4

Checker Weapons

Checkers is War and whenever you go to War it is smart to have as many weapons as possible. If, for example, you only have sticks and stones and a list of nasty names to call your enemy, you're in trouble! If he possesses guns, hand grenades, bazookas and flame throwers, and you go to battle then you better have a large supply of bandages, stretchers and body bags.

In this chapter you will learn about some simple but effective weapons (tricks) that you can use against your adversary. They are easy to learn and with a little practice, you can be knocking your enemy dead and win war after war.

Start by learning and understanding how to do the:
- A.   Sandwich move
- B.   Snake Eyes trick
- C.   Hippo Eyes trick
- D.   Three Musketeers Ambush
- E.   Two Musketeers Ambush
- F.   The King Sandwich move
- G.   The four Back Whack positions

Study these positions so that they become as automatic as a cat running up a tree at the sound of barking dogs coming after him. Remember the fable about the cat and fox being chased by the hounds. If you haven't heard it, it goes like this;

Once upon a time, a fox and a cat were resting under a tree when they heard the sound of hounds coming toward them. The cat quickly climbed up the tree and hid. This was the only trick he knew and he did it perfectly every time. He then called down to the fox, "Wise fox, what trick are you going to use to get away from the hounds"? The fox, who was always bragging about his many skills said, "Well let me think about it. I could use my 'climb on top of the fence trick', or my 'wade into the stream trick' to make them lose my scent, or maybe I'll use my 'double back on the same trail trick'. It's hard to choose as I have dozens of different tricks to choose from, I just don't know which one is best to use today". As he thought and thought, the hounds got closer and closer. Finally, the hounds were so close that all he could do was 'run', but it was too late. While the cat safely watched from high in the tree, the hounds caught his friend, the fox, and the story ends.

There is a lesson to be learned here and that is "Better to have one trick that you know well and use it at the right time, than to have twenty that you don't". Having a flamethrower in your arsenal is useless if you don't know how to light the flame, right? There have been hundreds of checker books written containing thousands of tricks, traps and puzzles. It would take decades to learn them all, however if you just make using the simple weapons taught in this chapter as automatic in your mind as tying your shoelaces, you'll be a dangerous warrior. So begin your weapons training today.

"There's more to Checkers than pushing plastic"

The Sandwich Move

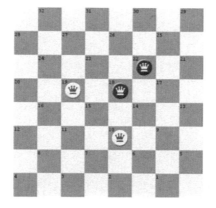

Figure 1 - RED to move and win

RED sees that by moving between the WHITE Kings he will gain a material advantage since WHITE can only move one of his Kings.

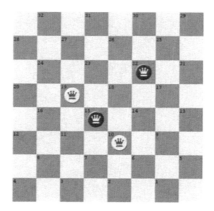

Figure 2 RED wins

Snake Eyes

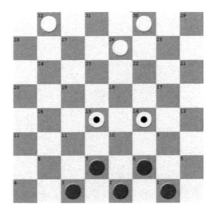

Figure 3 RED to move and win

By moving either 6-10 or 7-10, RED will get two Checkers for the price of one and hold a winning advantage.

Snake Eyes

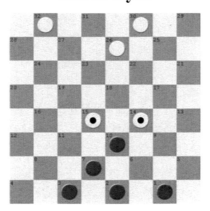

Figure 4 RED moves 6-10

Hippo Eyes

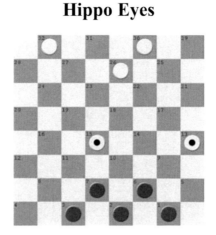

Figure 5 RED to move and win

RED gets to jump two Checkers after sacrificing the RED checker on square 6.

Hippo Eyes

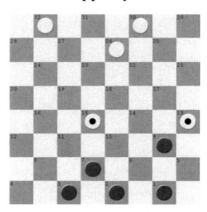

Figure 6 RED makes the winning move

Three Musketeer Ambush

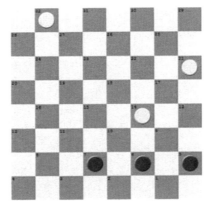

Figure 7 RED to move and win

RED can steal the man on square 14 by moving from 6 to 9. If he tries 6-10 WHITE will just take the trade.

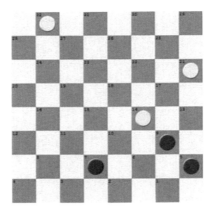

Figure 8 RED makes the winning move

Two Musketeer Ambush

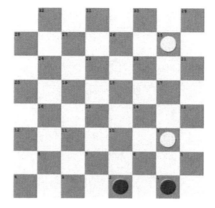

Figure 9 RED to move and win

Once again, RED can steal a man and hold a material advantage.

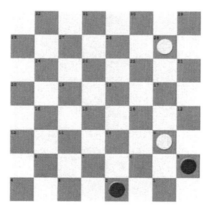

Figure 10 RED makes the winning move

The King Sandwich

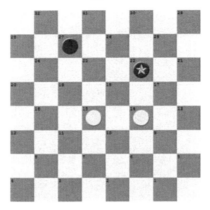

Figure 11 RED to move and win

Don't be too anxious to get a King, go for the material advantage and win.

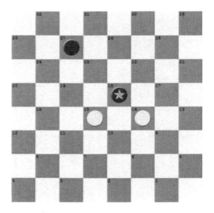

Figure 12 RED makes the winning move

Back Whack A

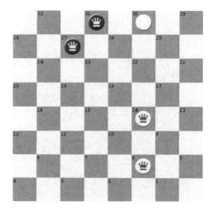

Figure 13 RED to move and win

Back Whack B

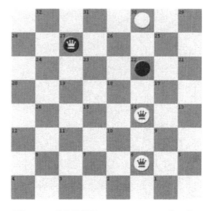

Figure 14 RED to move and win

Back Whack C

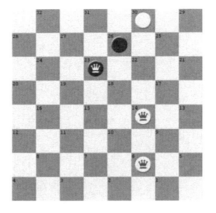

Figure 15 RED to move and win

Back Whack D

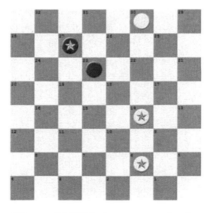

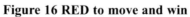

Figure 16 RED to move and win

In each of the above positions RED will sacrifice one checker and take three Checkers. See if you can find the winning move in all four positions before looking at the solutions below.

Remember, only a King can jump backward.

The winning moves are:
A. 31-26 - B. 22-26 - C. 23-27 - D. 23-26

The Highway

Figure 17– The Highway

This is the safe refuge; a King on the highway can't be trapped on the side of the board.

Advanced Weapons Training

Now that you've learned how to use a knife, sword and spear, it's time to develop your skills with more complicated arms. Learning to use a rifle, bazooka and flame thrower will take time and practice, but it's worth the effort.

First memorize the "Eleven to Heaven" (see figure 18) series of forced moves. Whenever your opponent has one King and you have two Kings, he will run down the "Highway" (see Figure 17) and hide in the double corner "Closet" believing that you can't get him out. You can! It takes exactly eleven moves starting from the position in figure 18 and there is no escaping from death once you start your attack.

Eleven to Heaven

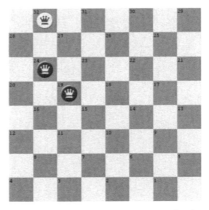

Figure 18 - RED to move and win

RED wins by forcing WHITE out of the Double Corner (closet) with 24 to 28, now WHITE must move 32-27. RED keeps up the force with 28-32 and now WHITE must move off the "Highway" 27-31. Next RED makes a move that seems to let WHITE go with 19-15, then 31-26, 15-18, 26-31, 18-22, 31-26 (or

31-27 same result) 22x31 (capture moves are designated with x instead of – separating the square numbers) and the game is over in just (count them) eleven moves.

Next master how to win when you have three Kings and he has two Kings. If both Kings are in opposite Closets on the highway, the "Thirty Seven to Heaven" sequence of moves guarantees a victory by forcing either the "Five on Seven" or Five on Seven Sister" positions.

Thirty Seven to Heaven

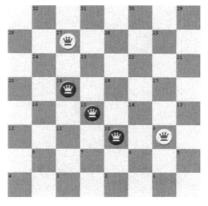

Figure 19 RED to win in 37 moves.

RED starts the winning sequence by moving his middle King (in this case that is the King on 15) forward so it is on the same diagonal as the 2 WHITE Kings.

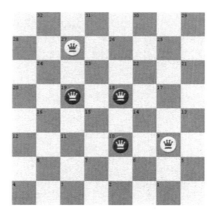

Figure 20 Position after 15-18.

This is to be prepared to take a trade in two moves if the WHITE side moves wrong, in which event the win can be accomplished in fewer moves. WHITE must now move one of his Kings (either one) into the double corner to avoid being trapped on the side of the board. RED then moves his King at that side of the board toward the King that the WHITE side has just moved. This results in the following position.

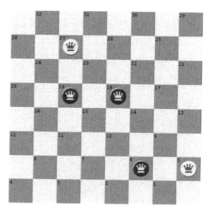

Figure 21 Position after 9-5 and 10-6.

Now WHITE must move his other King into the opposite double corner because RED will force a trade if the same WHITE King moves behind the RED King. This brings about the following position.

Figure 22 Position after 27-32.

Now the RED King moves from 19 to 23 and the WHITE King must move 5-1 to avoid the trade via 6-9 if the other King were moved.

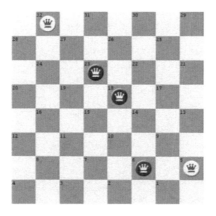

Figure 23 after RED's 19-23 move.

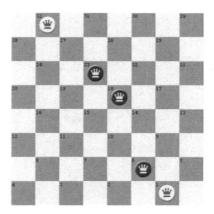

Figure 24 after WHITE's 5-1 move.

The RED King now moves 6-9 to be able to force a trade after the next move.

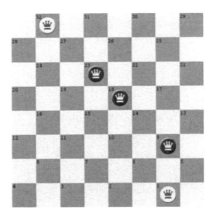

Figure 25 RED moved 6-9.

At this point WHITE has 2 possible moves, either 1-5 or 32-28.

If WHITE moves 1-5 RED moves 9-14 and forces a trade on the next move because WHITE cannot move both Kings and the un-moved King will be traded off.

Five on Seven position

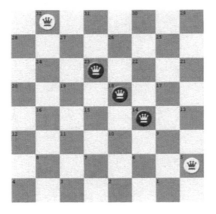

Figure 26 after the 1-5 and 9-14 moves.

Notice that RED will either trade by 23-27 or 14-9 and trade off the un-moved King.

Had WHITE moved 32-28 instead of 1-5, RED moves 23-27 and will bring about the following position.

Five on Seven Sister

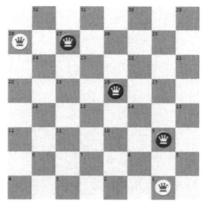

Figure 27 after 32-28 and 23-27.

Notice that WHITE must move either 1-5 or 28-32 and the King will be traded off.

If WHITE had moved 28-32

Figure 28 RED moves 9-14.

Now WHITE jumps 32x23 and RED jumps 18x27.

If WHITE had moved 1-5

Figure 29 Then RED moves 27-23.

Now WHITE jumps 5x14 and RED jumps 18x9.

After this sequence RED can win by forcing the "Eleven to Heaven" position for a total of 37 moves as follows.

1.	15-18	2.	9-5
3.	10-6	4.	27-32
5.	19-23	6.	5-1
7.	6-9	8.	32-28
9.	23-27	10.	1-5
11.	27-23	12.	5x14
13.	18x9	14.	28-24
15.	9-14	16.	24-28
17.	14-18	18.	28-24
19.	18-15	20.	24-28
21.	15-19	22.	28-32
23.	19-24	24.	32-28
25.	23-19	26.	28-32
27.	24-28	28.	32-27
29.	28-32	30.	27-31
31.	19-15	32.	31-26
33.	15-18	34.	26-31
35.	18-22	36.	31-26

37.   22x31 RED jumps WHITE's last remaining checker.

The game is over in exactly 37 moves against WHITE's best moves.

Instead of trying to commit the moves to memory, it is best to understand the ideas involved. On each move, the side with three Kings (RED in this case) threatens an exchange and in avoiding these exchanges WHITE is finally forced into the "Five on Seven" or "Five on Seven Sister" position.

If WHITE has both of his Kings in the same double corner "Closet" and you have three Kings, then use the "Twins in the Closet" sequence of moves as follows.

Twins in the Closet

Figure 30 RED to move and win.

From this position, RED starts the sequence by moving 17-14. This appears to give WHITE the 6-9 "Snake Eyes" two for one, but this would leave WHITE off the "Highway" and the King on square 5 can trap the WHITE King on the side of the board. That leaves WHITE's only move 6-2, then RED keeps up the attack with 13-9. WHITE now moves 1-6 (if 2-7, RED will trade with 14-10) and RED just lets WHITE jump the Checker on square 9 by moving 5-1. WHITE thinks "What is this dummy doing?" After 6x13, RED trades again 14-9, 13x6, 1x10 and the WHITE King on square 2 faces certain death.

Chapter 5

Checkers Armor and Shields

Defense

In checker tournaments, if you lose a game you receive a "bladeless knife without a handle". In other words, you get nothing, no points, zippo, no score, nada.

However, if you tie or draw a game, you get a blade for the first tie and the handle for the second draw. You see, a draw is worth one point and two draws scores the same as if you win a game, which is worth two points. So, if you're playing and can't clearly see a victory, then go for the draw. Half a candy bar is better than none, right?

Your biggest enjoyment in Checkers comes from winning. The second most enjoyable experience comes from drawing when you're 1, 2 or even 3 Checkers behind (see figures 35 & 36). This drives your opponent crazy and starts his tears flowing. So learn these drawing positions and use them to salvage a point from a losing game. There are numerous defensive tricks in Checkers. The simplest is to run your one and only King down the highway (Figure 17) to a double corner closet and hide if you don't have the "move". His lone King can't get to you. Having the "move" means that your lone King can pin your opponents lone King on the side of the board. A lone King on the "Highway" cannot be pinned by an opponent's lone King. This hide in the double corner trick also works with two Kings against two Kings. Keeping your Kings together in the closet is always smart. It even helps if he has three Kings against your two. Sometimes you can get a draw if he makes just one mistake. If he doesn't know the exact sequence of moves to force a trade, you can drive him nuts trying to do so and eventually he may concede a draw.

A good defensive position is a must in Checkers. Only a buffoon or dope runs around a boxing ring holding his hands behind his back. Doing so will shortly bring on a bloody nose. In Checkers, not keeping your bridge (Checkers on squares 1 and 3) as long as possible can also cause damage. With a bridge position it is not possible for your opponent to get a King without at least 2 Checkers. Keeping these men in place is like keeping your hands up in boxing. Using these two Checkers and some help from their friends, you can many times pull off the draw as shown on the following pages.

"There's more to Checkers than pushing plastic"

Meatless Sandwich

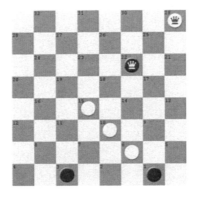

Figure 31 RED to move and draw.

RED takes the meat out of the sandwich by moving 3-7, 10x3, 1x10x19.

Meatless Pizza

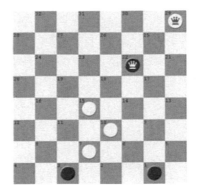

Figure 32 RED to move and draw.

RED plays 1-6, 10x1, 3x10x19 and draws.

The Vault

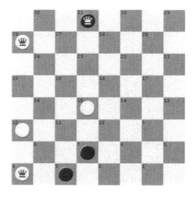

Figure 33 RED to move and draw.

Moving 7-11, 15x8 followed by 31-27 draws.

In and Out

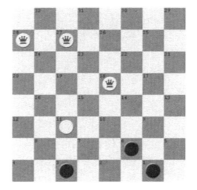

Figure 34 RED to move and draw.

RED draws by 3-7, 11x2, 1-5, 2x9, 5x14x23x32.

Tie and Cry

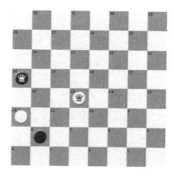

Figure 35 RED to move and draw

RED will lose a man and still draw with 8-11, 15x8 then 20-16 and RED will hold 2 WHITE Kings in the single corner by keeping his one King on squares 11 and 16.

Locked in the Closet

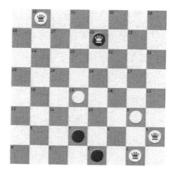

Figure 36 RED to move and draw

RED sacrifices 7-10 followed by 26-23 and draws three men short.

Chapter 6

Challenging Puzzles
and
Points to Ponder

The following puzzles illustrate some of the millions of possibilities that do arise in actual games if you play to allow them. Try to solve the problems for a few minutes before looking at the solutions at the back of this chapter.

Puzzle 1

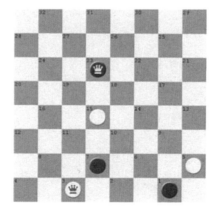

Figure 37 RED to move and win.

In this puzzle, RED appears to be losing as the man on square 7 cannot be rescued. Look for a way that RED can hold two WHITE pieces with just one King.

How to Throw Snowballs

Hitting a friend with a snowball is easy if you know how. You can't do it by just throwing one at him from 80 feet away, he'll simply move to the left or right. So, the trick is to divert his attention away from your attack.

Here's how to do it. First make two snowballs. Take one and throw it as high as possible aiming it to drop from above on his head. As he is looking up watching this high arcing snowball and thinking how dumb you are to believe he can't sidestep away from it, throw the second in a hard line drive trajectory straight at his chest. He'll never see it coming.

In Checkers you do the same trick of diverting his attention by moving your checker from square 4 out of the King row early in the game. This makes him think he can easily get a King in this corner. He will try to attack that empty square abandoning the center of the board.

Now you have control of the center (top of the hill) as well as an extra soldier to engage in the battle. This can often give you a winning advantage. So, just like throwing snowballs, first *divert*; then *attack.*

"There's more to Checkers than pushing plastic"

Puzzle 2

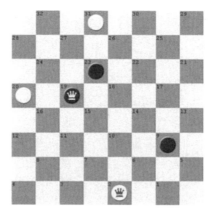

Figure 38 RED to move and win.

RED can force WHITE into a two for two "Back Whack" in just two moves. Then RED's King will trap the remaining WHITE man in the single corner.

Puzzle 3

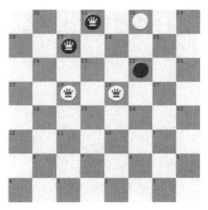

Figure 39 RED to move and win.

RED sacrifices a man to get a winning "Tail Hold".

Checkers then Chess

For a golfer, tennis player or baseball pitcher, which is more important, <u>POWER</u> or <u>ACCURACY</u>? The answer is neither. Being able to throw a baseball at 103 miles per hour is worthless if you can't get the ball over the plate. Hitting a golf ball perfectly down the middle of the fairway every time is inefficient if you can only drive the ball a maximum of 42 yards. Both power and accuracy are needed to be a "top-notch" player in these games. So, which quality should be obtained first? It has been proven that the proper sequence is for the young body to develop power <u>first</u>, then accuracy. It is wrongful thinking to reverse this order - just like mixing acid and water - you should always pour the acid into the water, never the other way around. Doing so could leave you with a steamed - <u>scarred face</u> for life.

Consequently, there is a right and wrong order in developing a young mind, as there is in developing a young body. The appropriate choice is to learn <u>Checkers</u> before <u>Chess</u>. Why? Becoming knowledgeable at playing Checkers is unquestionably a superior way for children to develop forethought.

For an example – Recently my 7 year old Grandson was playing Checkers against his 9 year old brother. He had three Kings on squares 10, 15 and 19, while his brother had Kings on the 9 and 27 squares. The 7 year old announced, "In 37 moves I'll be in Heaven." He recognized the position and knew that within 37 moves he would win regardless of anything his brother could do. Such an announcement has never been uttered from any Chess Grand Master, but a well trained 7 year old checker player can make such a prediction. This ability to think ahead is best cultivated and nourished while a person is young. This fact was well known in Russia during the 50's when they made it mandatory for chess prodigies to study <u>Checkers</u> beforehand. As a result, they've produced the largest number of Chess Grand Masters in the world.

If you want to have a strong endgame in chess, you will be well advised to first study Checkers. They need to be combined for maximum greatness, just as power and accuracy need to be.

"There's more to Checkers than pushing plastic"

Puzzle 4

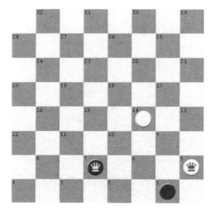

Figure 40 RED to move and win.

RED freezes two WHITE pieces in five moves.

Puzzle 5

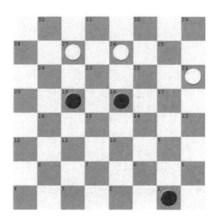

Figure 41 RED to move and win.

RED forces a "Snake Eyes" in five moves with a little help from WHITE. This illustrates the importance of proper timing.

Show Good Sportsmanship

Even though Checkers is a game of war, there are "do's" and "don'ts" to be followed. The proper protocol or Code-of-Conduct shows your opponent that you're not a primitive barbarian, even if you look and smell like one.

For example:

While you're waiting for your opponent to go, don't...

A. Fake snoring
B. Ask him if his father was a snail or lazy sloth.
C. Read a newspaper while singing "Any Day Now"
D. Keep looking at and tapping your wristwatch to see if it is still running.
E. Say, "Hey turtle brain, are you awake? Do you know it's your move?"

Instead spend your time looking for how this enemy is trying to attack you and how to best defend against this attack. Always remember to think <u>defense</u> first – and <u>offense</u> second. You'll lose more games because of what you <u>don't</u> see than by what you <u>do</u> see.

When it's your turn to move, don't...

A. Say, "I gotcha now, Bozo."
B. Say, "It's all over now but the crying" after slamming your piece down hard.
C. Ask him if he'll take a draw (when you're four Checkers down).
D. Do anything that may distract or annoy the attention of your opponent. Doing so is against the rules.

"There's more to Checkers than pushing plastic"

Be a Wonderful Loser

"Wonderful people" often use a "Wonderful Phrase". That phrase is "You're Welcome". However, in order for them to state this phrase someone else must first say "Thank You".

How do you get someone to say "Thank You"? Well you must first please them. One way to do that is to compliment them.

If you just lost your game, phrases like-

    A. "Nice game, you played well".

or —

    B. "You certainly made some brilliant moves today".

are pleasing for others to hear. Try being so gracious with your words after losing that your opponent will say "Thank You". If he does, you can reply, "You're Welcome" and walk away knowing you're becoming a wonderful person, even in defeat.

"There's more to Checkers than pushing plastic"

Puzzle 6

Figure 42 RED to move and win.

Look for a way to force "Hippo Eyes", then jump four WHITE Kings.

Puzzle 7

Figure 43 RED to move and win.

RED locks WHITE in the "Vault".

Knowing the End from the Beginning

One day my grandson asked me, "Granddad, if people can do whatever they choose, how can God know for sure how things will end"?

That's a good question, so to help explain this puzzling inquiry, I set up my checkerboard. I placed 3 single Checkers on the board numbering them #1, #2 and #3. Next, I placed my Checkers, 6 Kings on the board and announced "In exactly 16 moves from now, I will win regardless of anything you choose to do."

He moved first, choosing a checker and also deciding which way it should go. I then made my move. He again chose a checker and moved it according to his will, not mine. I then made my move. He continued to select a checker to move and designated it's advancement without any input from me. This continued until the game ended and I had won in exactly 16 moves, just as I had predicted from the beginning.

I then explained to him that I was able to do this because I knew the rules of the game, I had superior force and most important, I had knowledgeable foresight.

I asked him, "If a worm had witnessed what I just did – predicting the end from the beginning – what do you think it would say?" He answered, "The worm would say – "*INCONCEIVABLE*" (this is a word he learned from the movie "the Princess Bride")".

"Well, our minds are like a worm's compared to God", I explained, "and I hope this little demonstration helped to answer your question?" It did!

"There's more to Checkers than pushing plastic"

Puzzle 8

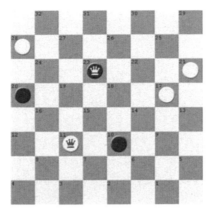

Figure 44 RED to move and win.

Just another "Back Whack" with a twist. Look for the winning sacrifice.

Puzzle 9

Figure 45 RED to move and win.

Look for a way to jump all four WHITE Checkers.

Keeping Mental Youthfulness

Many Grand Master Checker players are in their 70's and 80's which, is rarely the case for Chess players. Why is that?

Checker players develop a much greater ability to think ahead (forethought) than do Chess players. Even the great Chess Grand Master Jose' Raul Capablanca of Cuba was quoted as saying "I see only <u>one</u> move ahead, but it's always the correct one." Checker experts think dozens, or more moves ahead.

Researchers, using MagnetoEncePhalography, have shown that playing Checkers, not chess, drastically increases the brain's "Medial Temporal Lobe" activity. Maybe this explains the reason checker players stay so strong mentally for so long.

Retirement homes would certainly benefit from having weekly checker tournaments and turning off the "boob tube".

"There's more to Checkers than pushing plastic"

Puzzle 10

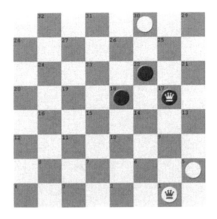

Figure 46 RED to move and win.

Try to find a way for RED to lock the two WHITE pieces in the "Closet".

Puzzle 11

Figure 47 RED to move and win.

RED can win with one King against two Kings and a man by using this clever trick.

Unpaid Walking Billboards

It seems to me that today's teen-agers have more "cents" than (common) "sense". I'll explain….. Over a half century ago, when I was young, there were two types of people who walked around in public promoting a product. The first were usually behemoth size men who paraded the streets wearing a sign that read "I buy my clothes at Watershed's Clothing Store for Big and Tall men". We called him "Sandwich Man".

The second were team members like a girl's softball team, whose jerseys read "Select Laundry, Inc.". Both had enough brains (sense) to be receiving some sort of "financial gain" (cents) for their advertising efforts.

This was during a period in America when Checkers ruled all other games. In general, these folks had fewer "cents" compared to today's individuals, but seemed to have more "sense". Why do I say this? Today's young, keyboard tickling, computer geeks buy clothing advertising things like Nintendo™, X-box™, Old Navy™, Nike™, Gameboy™, etc., then walk around in public for free. That makes no <u>sense</u> or <u>cents</u> for them, but dollars for the companies. Kids are becoming an army of chattel and free "walking bill-boards". In fact, these product manufacturers have duped and bamboozled our young people to not only become their "advertising slaves", but have tricked them into paying for this privilege. How absurd! Good checker players don't fall for such "subtle traps", either "on-the-board" or in "real life".

"There's more to Checkers than pushing plastic"

Puzzle 12

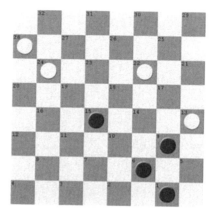

Figure 48 RED to move and win.

Make a slip and the slaughter will follow.

Puzzle 13

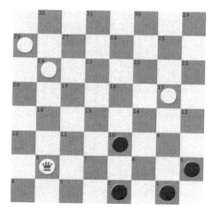

Figure 49 RED to move and win.

Try to force the same type of ending as Puzzle 12.

Dog Dirt Lesson

When I was nine years old, I was sitting on the back step in our yard scraping dog-dirt off the bottom of my shoe with a stick.

My checker playing dad came out of the door and noticed what I was doing and asked, "Stepped in dog-dirt did you son?" "Yes", I replied.

He then stated, "Well, son, don't worry about it, we've all done that same thing in our lives." That made me feel better. He then added, "Now, remember not to step in that same pile a <u>second</u> time. If you do, it means your brain isn't working, O.K.?"

He started walking away, as I pondered his wise advice. Moments later he came back and said, "One more thing son, if you step in that same pile a <u>third</u> time, Do me a favor. Don't tell anyone that I'm your dad, O.K.?"

That advice is wise both in life and in playing Checkers. Try hard not to repeat your earlier mistakes.

"There's more to Checkers than pushing plastic"

Puzzle 14

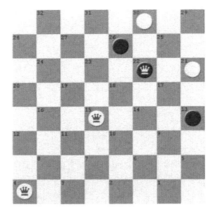

Figure 50 RED to move and win.

Puzzle 15

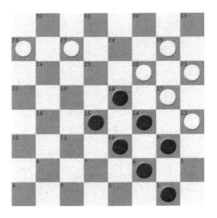

Figure 51 RED to move and win.

Earnings

$$\updownarrow$$

Yearnings

The greatest financial advice I know is to "Keep your yearnings below your earnings". In other words; if you drive up to a gas station in your brand new $60,000 Hummer and you can't afford to fill it up with gasoline, then you're driving the wrong car. Such a person probably isn't a good checker player because he lacks foresight.

Sometimes in Checkers, you are blinded by your "yearning" to get a checker up on your opponent, that you fail to see the disastrous future. As you can see in this position, RED can seemingly steal the WHITE checker on square 9 by moving 1-5.

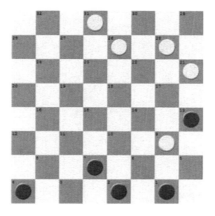

Figure 52 RED to move.

This would be disastrous for RED because WHITE will move 25-22 and be in a position to take 3 RED Checkers for one of his own; after RED jumps 5-14 WHITE will move 22-17, then 13-22 then WHITE jumps from 26 over 3 Checkers to square 3.

What appears to be a free checker (one you did not earn) will cost you dearly down the road.

A Hummer with little gas will not go very far. A player who does not think defensively before thinking offensively will not go far in a tournament.

Remember, when it's your turn to move and you suddenly see a "great move", sit on your hands. Why? Because you are not thinking defensively first and his "gift" could be a trap.

Bob Murr and his grandson

"There's more to Checkers than pushing plastic"

Puzzle Solutions

1. RED moves 23-19, 3x10, 1-6, 10x1, 19x10 and WHITE can't move (loses).

2. Push 9-14, 2-6, (or 2-7 loses the same way – try it) 23-26, 31x22, 14-18, 22x15, 19x10x1 RED wins.

3. Move 22-26, 30x23, 31-26 and WHITE must move a King and then lose a man and a King.

4. RED makes a winning combination, 1-6, 5-1, 6-9, 14x5, 7-10 RED wins.

5. Move 1-6, 21-17, 6-10, 17-13, 10-14, now WHITE gives RED the backing he needs to win by 13-9, 18-23, 27x18, 14x23x30.

6. Sacrifice the RED King 23-18, 14x23, (see the "Hippo Eyes"?) now 5-9, 13x6, 1x10x19x26x17 and it's all over but the shouting.

7. RED sacrifices two men with 15-18, 22x15x8, (WHITE blocks his own King) 6-10, 3-7, 10x3 and RED wins, WHITE being unable to move.

8. RED can't win if he takes the "two for one" (20-24, 28x19, 23x16x7, 17-14, 10x17 and 21x14 draws.) RED makes it a "three for two" instead with 10-14, 17X10, now 20-24, 28x19, 23x16x7x14 RED wins.

9. RED starts the ball rolling with 27-24, 28x19, and continues with 26-23, 19x26, and clears the board, 30x23x14x7x16.

10. RED ends WHITE's misery with 22-26, 30x23x14, and 17x10.

11. RED sacrifices the man 2-7, 10x3, 16-12, now WHITE's only move is 3-7, 12x3x10 and traps the remaining King in the single corner.

12. RED goes 6-10 the "Slip", 13x6, 15-18 now the "slaughter" 22x15, 10x19,24x15 and 1x10x19 now the funeral.

13. RED pressures WHITE by moving 5-9, WHITE can't let RED just ambush the man on 17, so he moves 17-13. This provides RED with the proper timing to move 2-7, 13x6, 7-11, 8x15, 10x19, 24x15, 1x10x19. Notice the similarity to Puzzle 12.

14. RED loses if he just goes for the King, but has this beautiful winning combination. 13-17, 21x14, (if WHITE jumps 30x23, then 22-26 will win) 22-17, 30x23, 17x10x19x26 and wins by trapping WHITE's King off the Highway.

15. RED begins the fireworks with 15-19, 22x15, 19-23, 27x18, 10x19, 17x10, 6x15x22x29, 13x6, 1x10, 21-17, 29-25 and wins with overwhelming material and positional advantage.

Chapter 7

Standard Rules of Checkers

1.   The checkerboard to be used in official matches and tournaments shall be green and buff (off white) with two-inch squares. The board shall be placed for playing so that the green single corner is on the left side and the double corner is on the right-hand side.

2.   The Checkers to be used in official matches and tournaments shall be Red and White in color, round, and of a diameter not less than one and one-quarter inches nor more than one and one-half inches. The pieces shall be placed on the green squares.

3.   At the beginning of the contest, the players shall draw for colors. The player having the Red Checkers shall make the first move. Thereafter, the players shall alternate in leading off with Red in each succeeding game.

4.   The men move diagonally forward, one space at a time, to an unoccupied adjacent dark square in the row ahead. If there is an opponent's checker or King on an adjacent square in the row ahead with an unoccupied square on the same diagonal line in the following row, that piece (checker or King) must be jumped and removed from the board. The checker or King continues jumping if possible until all jumps are completed. The jumped pieces are removed after all of the jumps are completed, then it is the opponents turn to move.

5.   Players are allowed up to 5 minutes to study the board if necessary and then no more than one minute to complete the move. If a player fails to move in the allotted time, the game shall be adjudged as lost through improper delay.

6.	When there are two or more ways to jump, five minutes shall be allowed for the move. When there is only one way to jump, time shall be called at the end of one minute, and if the move is not completed at the end of another minute, the game shall be adjudged as lost through improper delay.

7.	Special time rules can apply at some tournaments (such as the use of time clocks specifying a given number of moves in a given time) to speed up play in certain situations. Usually 30 moves are required to be completed in 1 hour.

8	If a player has more than one way to jump, he may select whichever one he wants, regardless of the number and type of pieces that can be captured.

9.	After the game has started, if either player touches or arranges any piece without first giving notice, he shall be warned for the first offense and shall forfeit the game for any subsequent offense of this kind. If a person whose turn it is to play touches one of his playable pieces, he must either play it or forfeit the game.

10.	If any part of a playable piece is played over an angle of the square on which it is stationed, the play must be completed in that direction. Inadvertently removing, touching, or disturbing from its position a piece that is not playable, while in the act of jumping or making an intended move, does not constitute a move, and the piece or pieces shall be placed back in position and the game continued.

11.	When a checker reaches the King row of the board by reason of a move or as the completion of a jump, it becomes a King. That completes the move or jump. The opponent must then crown the checker by placing a piece on top of it. The King can then continue jumping if possible on its next move. The opponent must crown the King before making a move. When a piece is not available for crowning, the referee must furnish one.

12.   A King once crowned can move and jump forward and backward.

13.   A draw is declared when the players agree the game cannot be won. When the players are not in agreement and one side appears stronger than the other, and the player with what appears to be the weaker side requests the referee for a count on moves, then, if the referee so decides, the stronger party is required to complete the win, or to show to the satisfaction of the referee at least an "increased" advantage over his opponent within 40 of his own moves, these to be counted from the point at which notice was given by the referee. If he fails to do this, he must relinquish the game as a draw.

14.   A game is won when the opponent is unable to move, either because all of his pieces have been jumped and removed or he is blocked and unable to move.

15.   Any spectator giving warning either by signs or sound or remark on any of the games, whether playing or pending, shall be ordered from the room during the contest. Play shall be discontinued until such offending party retires. Spectators shall not be allowed to talk near the playing boards.

Chapter 8

Moving to the Next Level

In this chapter I will give you some information to help you reach the "expert" level in Checkers.

Websites

The first internet website you should know about is the official American Checker Federation (ACF).

http://www.usacheckers.com

Here you find a lot of information about Checkers and the players. There is a store where you can buy official Checkers and Boards as well as books. I am sure that you will enjoy exploring this exciting website.

Other informational and interesting places to visit and explore are:

http://www.fierz.ch/checkers.htm

This is the website of Martin Fierz, creator of "CheckerBoard", the **free** download Checker program that plays Checkers at the Master level. The diagrams in this book were created using Martin's program. This is one of the most useful creations ever to help learn and study the game of Checkers.

http://www.jimloy.com/checkers/checkers.htm

This website is chock full of historical games and analysis as well as problems and stories. Jim Loy has done an outstanding job in building and maintaining this important website. Jim Loy is also the editor of the ACF Bulletin.

http://www.checkermaven.com

The Checker Maven website is due to the terrific efforts of Bob Newell. Mr. Newell puts a lot of effort into keeping his site updated and making sure the information is correct. He has book reviews, all sorts of downloads of books no longer in print, as well as Checker program reviews, etc. Be sure to visit his site weekly as he updates on Saturdays with new problems and stories. Check out all of his links.

http://www.nccheckers.org

This is the official site of the North Carolina Checker Association. J. R. Smith does a fantastic job of keeping this website current. It has interesting stories and Checker news of both upcoming tournaments and results of completed tournaments. I know you will enjoy this interesting and informative website.

http://www.dailyspeculations.com/Letter/wiswell.htm

Victor Niederhoffer has provided this site as a tribute to former World Champion Checker Player, Tom Wiswell. Mr. Wiswell had a splendid way with words and many of his proverbs are enshrined in the beautiful website.

Mr. Niederhoffer holds a lifetime membership in the ACF and is a major contributor to the ACF Youth Foundation making a $5000 contribution to the prize fund of the 2007 ACF Arthur Niederhoffer Youth Tournament.

Playing Others on the Web

There are many internet game playing sites frequented by many very good Checker players.

Here is a partial list:

http://www.goldtoken.com (Official ACF site)
http://www.kurnik.org
http://www.itsyourturn.com
http://games.yahoo.com/board-games
http://brainking.com/
http://www.wylliedraughts.com
http://board-games.pogo.com

This is certainly not a complete listing and I am sure that you will find your own favorite site. Some are live play while others are "turn based" and may take several days to complete a game as moves are sent and your opponent is notified by email that it is his turn to move.

Joining Checker Organizations

You can join the ACF on line by using the link at the top, right hand side of the home page. After joining the ACF, you will be eligible to enter ACF sponsored tournaments and also will receive a bi-monthly ACF news bulletin.

The Missouri Checker Association (MCA) is an organization that sends out a monthly newsletter and an annual roster of members. The ACF website provides the following link to the MCA.

http://www.usacheckers.com/mca.php

You can use this link to obtain the necessary information to join the MCA.

Acknowledgements

I take this opportunity to thank the following persons whose support and encouragement made this venture possible.

Robert L. Murr (Colorado State Checker Champion)

Alan Millhone (President of the American Checker Federation)

Martin Fierz (Developer of CheckerBoard, the program used to provide the Checker diagrams in this book)

To Order Copies of

How to Beat Granddad at Checkers

Revised Edition

by John P. Cardie
Illustrations by Bob Murr

I.S.B.N. 1-59879-390-X

Order Online at:
www.authorstobelievein.com

By Phone Toll Free at:
1-877-843-1007